Old Moffat

by

Emilio Dicerbo

At the junction of Chapel Brae and the Beattock to Moffat Road, the old toll cottage had been re-roofed by the time of this early twentieth-century view. The larger, more modern building on the left of the foreground is Annandale House, built around 1914 by the Annandale Estates to accommodate the estate factor and his family. The road curves off to the right, crosses two bridges and is then hidden from view by a row of mature beech trees as it nears Moffat railway station and the southern approach to the town. Only one of the bridges can be seen in this view; the other was part of an earlier flood prevention scheme and was replaced by a pipe in 1960 when the road was upgraded (although this later turned out to be inadequate for flood waters). The high church spire in the centre of the photograph belonged to the Old Well Road United Presbyterian church which was demolished in the early 1960s, only 100 years after its construction. Across the river, just above Annandale House, the Glebe is in its original state, a damp, rushy meadow. It has since been developed with bungalows.

First published in the United Kingdom, 2014,
by Stenlake Publishing Ltd.
01290 551122
www.stenlake.co.uk

Printed by Berforts, 17 Burgess Road, Hastings, TN35 4Nr
ISBN 9781840336528

Acknowledgements

The author would like to thank Adam Anderson, Anne Murray, Jim Storrar and the Moffat Museum for their assistance while writing this book

Further Reading

The books listed below were used by the author during his research. None of them is available from Stenlake Publishing. Those interested in finding out more are advised to contact their local bookshop or reference library.

Emilio Dicerbo *Memories of Moffat* 1999
Emilio Dicerbo *Memories of Moffat: Revised Edition* 2004
Emilio Dicerbo *Moffat Connections* 2010
W.R. Turnbull *History of Moffat* 1871

'The popular Scottish spa' and 'a charming holiday resort with bracing mountain air' is how Moffat was sold to tourists and visitors in the late 1800s and early 1900s. Illustrated on the cover of this brochure are views from Coate's Hill, Raehill's Glen, the Grey Mare's Tail, Garpol Glen and the Waterside Walk, all attractions that brought holidaymakers to the town. The brochure also advertised the available sporting facilities and pastimes, including golf, tennis, croquet and bowls. Angling was featured too, with special mention of the rivers and the fish that could be caught in them. Distances to larger towns and cities were also listed, with beauty spots and places of historical interest described, together with travel times and transport available.

Introduction

The name 'Moffat' is said to be derived from the Gaelic *oua-vat*, a long, deep mountain hollow, or from the Irish *Mai-fad*, the 'long plain'. The original site of the town was probably at Alton (from the Scots for 'auld toon'), a short distance to the north-east of the town's present location and where the Knights Templar farmed and had a small chapel in the twelfth century.

When the Romans came to this region at the beginning of the first century they called the people *Selgovae*, 'The Hunters', but the *Selgovae* do not appear to have been a fierce tribe. Once conquered, they settled down into a sort of friendship with the Romans while others went to join the Scots and the Picts further north.

The invaders remained in Upper Annandale for four hundred years and the two most obvious signs of Roman occupation in the area that remain are the remnants of forts and the routes of roads. In 1900 traces of the ruins of fifty Roman fortlets were recorded throughout Upper Annandale.

Soon after the Norman conquest of England in the eleventh century, the Bruce family came across the border to Dumfriesshire where they were granted Annandale by David I in 1124. There was a church by 1177 and around this time defensive towers and castles were built, including Lochwood.

By the mid 1500s there was much inter-clan rivalry between the powerful Johnstone and the Maxwell families who competed for the powerful political posts of 'Warden of the Western Marches' and the 'Stewardship of Annandale'. Raiding and plundering were commonplace on both sides with each contender having support from other clans, leading to the inevitable ending on 7 December 1593. In the last clan battle fought in Scotland, at Dryfe Sands just north of Lockerbie, the Crichtons and Maxwells were defeated by the Johnstones, Elliots, Scotts and Grahams.

In 1633 the discovery of the Moffat mineral well by Rachel Whiteford would eventually bring thousands of visitors to the town. However, before that the area had to endure the misery of the 'Killing Times' which for the area began in 1638 when Rachel's father, minister of Moffat kirk since 1610, was ordered to introduce the new Episcopalian service. Being staunch Presbyterians, Moffat residents objected strongly and Whiteford was forced to leave the town shortly afterwards. In the 1680s John Graham of Claverhouse – 'Bluidy Clavers' – was ordered to quell all Covenanting activity in the district and he made his base at the Black Bull Hotel for three years, forcing the 'test oath' on the local population and brutally suppressing any religious dissent.

The eighteenth century was a more peaceful and prosperous time for the town and there was a post office by 1715. Another mineral well was discovered at Hartfell in the mid 1700s and from that time the establishment of hotels, mills and a new church were all testament to the town's growing prosperity. By the end of the century the population was about 800 and Moffat was firmly established as a spa town, a reputation reinforced by the opening of the Baths Hall (now the town hall) in 1827.

Later developments that century were the opening of the Beechgrove recreation grounds and the unveiling of the Colvin Fountain. Then in 1878 the Hydropathic Hotel opened and the number of coaches clattering along the Beechgrove increased dramatically, with a further increase by those travelling to and from the hotel when the Moffat railway station opened in April 1883. St Andrew's Church of 1790 was replaced by the present St Andrew's in 1878 and the Presbyterian Auld Kirk of 1843 at Annanside was replaced by St Mary's on Academy Road in 1893 (this building has been converted into luxury flats). The single-storey Moffat Academy of 1834 was replaced on the same site by an attractive two-storey building which is empty today and the late 1890s saw the development of Moffat's Station Park and boating pond.

By the century's end the population stood at nearly two and a half thousand and that is where it has more or less stayed ever since. By the end of the 1950s the town lost its railway passenger services and the Hydro had long-since burned down. Nonetheless, the town's popularity with tourists continued and there were a number of small hotels for visitors and plenty of shops, around fifty at that time. Today only eight of those remain trading the same wares, but plenty of others have opened up and Moffat remains a desirable place to live and a popular destination for daytrippers and holidaymakers.

Bordering the west side of the town, the River Annan used to wind its way towards the an area of marshy ground known as the 'Kerr' through the Annandale Field, the Glebe and grazing land. Around 1880, from a point near the cemetery, the river course was diverted to the much straighter route it follows today and this is the reason that the area now occasionally floods as the river, in raging spate, seeks out its old course. When the river was settled in its new course, the Glebe and beyond was still damp and was a perfect base on which to create a park with ponds. Thus, in the 1890s, the park and its three ponds were formed: the 'wee' pond, the 'middle' pond and the 'big' pond. Water feeds into the wee pond from a burn that borders the Annandale Field; it then runs into the middle pond, and from there runs into the big (boating) pond. This view of the boating pond, taken on a pleasant morning and featuring the boatman and a nanny with her charges, depicts only a fraction of Station Park and the attractions that made it so popular. Paths were laid to follow the contours of the ponds, flower beds were cultivated, a pavilion built and a putting green laid out. In the late 1940s the wee pond was lined with concrete and made suitable for paddling, becoming a very popular attraction throughout the summer for hundreds of children who frolicked in it with mothers seated close by, ready with towels, lemonade and tattie crisps. Mr Ewan Cameron was the first park keeper, boatman and gardener at Station Park but perhaps better-known was the jovial Bob Tweedie. Except for his war service, from the age of fifteen until the age of 72 Bob dedicated his life to maintaining the park, earning him the Queen's Medal for long service.

The southern end of the High Street, looking towards the old meal mill, *c*. 1873. Before the Bank of Scotland was built on its site in 1876, crofters brought their corn to be ground into flour at the mill. The road leading from the High Street to the left is Holm Street, accessing Holmend, the old Carlisle road and the Selkirk road. The entrance to Holm Street was only four yards across at this time, but shortly after the Second World War the houses on the left, bordering the old cemetery, were demolished down to the corner to widen the road as it is today. During the war these houses were used by the Royal Engineers, who booby-trapped the rooms inside in order to train officers and men at the battle school how to defuse them. The Annandale Hotel on the right was built as the King's Arms in 1762 (the name changed around 1864). A popular coaching inn, records from 1788 note that there was stabling for fifty horses. Four fresh horses could be hitched in fifty seconds and the speed of the journey increased from six to seven miles per hour. (Every coaching inn on the route from London to Edinburgh stabled horses and 620 were required for the journey.) In 1817 the Grand Duke Nicholas of Russia stayed at the King's Arms with his entourage. As it was the only small-town inn they found in Scotland where the whole party had their own bed to sleep in, they were greatly impressed. The chamberlain, Baron Nicolai, paid double the bill on leaving.

In the Bank of Scotland building, constructed from whinstone and sandstone, business activities were conducted on the ground floor while the two upper floors provided accommodation for the bank manager and his family. After 125 years the Bank of Scotland moved to smaller premises on the High Street. The horse-drawn station dray is being led by the station's carter, Mr Grierson, as he continues his delivery round of items brought in by train, while across the street is the delivery lorry of Armstrong and Dickie, mineral water manufacturers from Dumfries. The driver was probably dropping off an order to Crosbie's grocers and wine merchants or the Buccleuch public bar. Miller's shop on the left was later occupied by Swanston the ironmonger.

Left: Seen here in 1926, these two young children quench their thirst with a drink of water from one of the metal cups at the 'Ram', properly known as the Colvin Fountain. This bronze sculpture was funded by William Colvin of Craigielands, Beattock, at a cost of £600 and was donated to the town in 1875. The sculptor was William Brodie and the subject selected because of the close association between the town and sheep farming. Colvin was an iron industrialist and took up residence at Craigielands Estate in 1855 together with his sister and ailing mother who died in 1858. At the time of the unveiling of the fountain, Colvin was himself in ill health and was represented at the ceremony by his brother, Dr Robert Colvin from Edinburgh. Colvin died in 1880 and was buried in Beattock Cemetery. In March 2002 it was discovered that the fountain needed remedial work and the repairs were carried out in December 2003, with the Ram back on his cairn by March 2004. Fully restored, it is now floodlit, pumped water keeps its troughs filled and railings have been erected around it.

Right: The Armstrongs, Gentles, Browns and finally the Wallace Brothers since 1948 – over a hundred years of butchers trading from the same premises at the corner of the High street and Well Street. The shop is under the green clock tower and when the Armstrongs were the owners the clock would be in working order, striking the hours with its characteristic chime. However since 1952, when it was lowered to eradicate dry rot, it has been silent. Hygiene-wise, the display of meat in those far off days clearly left a lot to be desired! The carbide lamp on the bicycle was common enough; it was actually also a type favoured by salmon poachers as it shone a bright circular beam through the surface of the water, highlighting the fish.

The High Street around 1909. James Weatherhead, baker and confectioner, was succeeded in the premises on the right by the bakery business of the Reive family, then the Mitchells, and finally the Littles, who occupy it today. The tall building to the left of the baker's, standing between Henderson Street and Rae Street, contained George Young's grocers and wine merchants. In 1917 George moved across the street to the grocer's premises of John Young (no relation), next to Burnie's drapers (now the post office). Continuing down the High Street, after Young's is the Buccleuch Hotel, then the Buccleuch public bar, and finally Crosbie's grocers and wine merchants. The Buccleuch Hotel was originally the two-storey Rae's Inn, but in 1862 the enterprising Mrs Cranstoun sold the Annandale Arms Hotel to Mr Norris and bought and rebuilt the inn as a three-storey hotel, moving it back about four yards from the road. Crosbie's was also demolished and rebuilt on the corner of Church Place around 1900. The two-storey building between them contained the Buccleuch's dining room in the upper storey and the bar was in the lower. The coach parked outside the hotel is the 'Tibbie Shiels', which belonged to the hotel and was kept busy departing to or arriving from locations such as the station, the mineral well, the Grey Mare's Tail and Tibbie Sheil's Inn. The driver at the time of the photo was John Muir; a similar coach, the 'Ettrick Shepherd', was run by the Annandale Arms Hotel. The mineral well was a popular spot and at times two or even three coaches could arrive there at the same time, each having departed from their hotels at 7.15 a.m.

The Moffat-based firm of James Gibson and Son started in 1919 and from the early 1920s ran a regular and popular service between Moffat and Dumfries using a Ford Model T bus. The timetable remained unchanged for many years, so much so that townspeople and those who were picked up *en route* knew it off by heart. The buses also provided a delivery service between the two towns. By 1949 a double-decker had joined the Gibson fleet. For a number of years both Mr Gibson (Jimmy) and his brother Davy drove buses on a regular basis, with Davy's bus conspicuous with its 'Scotland Yet' emblem on the radiator. The 1970s saw the end of the driver/conductor combination on Gibson's buses and by that time there was a steady stream of organisations booking buses for tours, day trips and evening mystery runs. Following Jimmy Gibson's death in 1975, his grandson James and granddaughter Margaret continued to build up the business, eventually dropping school and service runs to concentrate on a range of weekend breaks and extended tours pioneered by their mother, Wilhelmina Margaret. The bus and coach fleet continued to change as the Gibsons maintained their reputation for up-to-date vehicles and by 2000 fourteen luxury coaches and minibuses were in constant use. Sadly, times changed as fuel prices rose, forcing the cost of tours beyond the means of those who had previously supported them, and after 88 years of helpful and courteous service 'Gibson's Buses' ceased trading. The bus office was based in Church Street for over fifty years.

Moffat High Street is 300 yards long by fifty yards wide, an extent perhaps more obvious when this photograph was taken around 1910. The first planting of the hybrid lime trees was around 1898 but these died by over-watering from dogs. The subsequent planting a year or so later was more successful as metal guards allowed them to flourish. Prominent on the right of this view are James Sinclair's grocers and Armstrong's butchers in the building with the clock tower on the opposite side of the entrance to Well Street. Dickson House, the two-storey house further up just beyond the lamp standard, was still at that time a dwelling house. It was built by James Dickson, the town's stamp master (postmaster) in 1772, but in 1934 the frontage was changed considerably when James Barr and Son moved to these premises from Well Street. Their attractive shop, The Treasure House of Moffat, was in business for over twenty years and stocked all manner of fancy goods, gifts and toys. Moffat Woollen Mill is now in the premises.

Left: On the east side of the High Street stands the Star Hotel, sited between Star Street and Mansfield Place. It was built in the 1700s as a two-storey establishment but in 1862 it had a complete makeover, including the addition of a third storey as there was no scope for adding any extra width. The hotel is 162 feet long but only twenty feet wide and it is recorded in the *Guinness Book of Records* as the narrowest hotel in Britain. A short distance from the end of the building, further along Star Street, is another Guinness record holder, Chapel Street, which links to Well Street and leads to the chapel and contains only one dwelling. At nine feet, eleven inches wide and eighteen feet, five inches long on its shorter side, it is recorded as the shortest street in Scotland. The chapel was originally Episcopalian and then became an Oddfellows' Hall before assuming its current role as St Luke's Roman Catholic Church.

Right: All the streets leading from the west side of the High Street were no more than narrow lanes: Henderson Street, Rae Street, Annangate, the Wide Close and Coutts Close. The Wide Close became Church Street when a building located where it joined the High Street was demolished and the United Free Church was built at Annanside in 1843, and Coutts Close – entered from the High Street between the Ariete Café and Gemini jewellers – is now named Syme Street. In 1900 this lane, which runs from the High Street to the road junction at the bottom of Church Street, ran between houses and a joiner's workshop. At that time there were no fewer than fourteen dwellings in Coutts Close and Annangate but with the demolition of most of the buildings a communal drying green and parking area now occupy the space. Only three feet wide, the tiny entry to the High Street is surely another contender for the *Guinness Book of Records*.

The provost and magistrates of Moffat – with the town band and Moffat Cadet Force attending – proclaim the accession of King George V at the Market Cross, 10 May 1910. There were no health and safety regulations in those days, as can be seen by the lack of scaffolding around the town clock. Tradesmen of the day carrying out remedial work or redecoration would have gained access to the precarious boardwalk by ladder. Armstrong's butchers adjoined the premises of George G. Grieve, grocer, through the arched entrance into the market place yard. On the other side of the entrance to Causeway Street from Grieve's was Miller's drapers, later to become the drapery of Thomas Fortune. Next to it, at the edge of the photograph, is Hetherington's chemists.

Mr Crosbie's grocer's and wine merchant's shop on the corner of Church Place and the High Street, pictured after it was rebuilt in the early 1900s. At that time there were another seven grocers and wine and spirit shops in the town. Compared with the number of grocers in Moffat today (two including the Co-op supermarket), eight is a bit of a surprise but even more surprising is the fact that in the mid-nineteenth century the townspeople supported fourteen grocers and thirteen boot and shoemakers. Crosbie's original shop was much smaller, with just one small window. The family sold the business to W. Harkness in the early 1960s and since that time the premises have contained an antiques shop, a baker's, a bicycle shop, a woollen goods shop and is currently the gift shop Present Time.

The war memorial was unveiled on 28 November 1920 by Dumfriesshire MP Major Murray of Murraythwaite Estate (near Dalton). At the unveiling, local residents and others from the outlying district who had lost relatives in the Great War were among the large crowd. The memorial lists 76 soldiers, sailors and RAF personnel killed in action (later joined by 16 more names from the Second World War and three from conflicts since then). It was originally built with six sections in the column but a great gale on 16 October 1949 blew over the tall pillar and it was rebuilt with only four sections. The 'wings' supporting the cross atop the pillar were originally part of the weather vane of St Andrew's Church which stood a little north-west of the present church between 1790 and 1887. The weather vane is known as the 'flying spur'; when it was on St Andrew's Church its wings were horizontal.

David Young, on the left, with his son Eric in their well-stocked grocer's shop. David's brother George was a purveyor of tea, wine and provisions who originally traded from premises between Henderson Street and Rae Street purchased from Nettleship grocers in 1901 (the shop is now a branch of Barnardo's). He moved to the premises seen here (now the Rumblin Tum), on the opposite side of the High Street, in 1917 and David took over the business after George's death. The shop remained in the family until Eric's retirement in 1974. Until the mid 1920s David Young, like most other wine merchants in the town, blended his own whisky, mixing four different fine highland whiskies together to produce his 'Annandale blend'.

The Annandale Hotel was originally known as the King's Arms and was the main coaching inn in the district. However, in 1822 the Beattock Bridge Hotel opened, more easily serving the recently opened Beattock to Elvanfoot road, and the King's Arms lost much of its business. It then provided room-and-kitchen lodging for poorer folk before failing completely. The building was then bought by the enterprising Mrs Cranstoun, owner of the Spur Inn on High Street (later the Balmoral Hotel), and she enlarged and refitted it, renaming it the Annandale Arms. She remained the owner until 1863, then sold it to Robert Norris and moved down to Rae's Inn which she completely rebuilt as the Buccleuch Hotel. As the nineteenth century progressed, coaching trade in the guise of excursion coaches became extremely popular and in this photograph from the late 1800s a touring coach, the 'Ettrick Shepherd', is about to depart from the hotel on a trip to St Mary's Loch. George Cavers, bedecked in his top hat, is the driver. At times three or four coaches would leave from the hotel at the same time, drawing crowds of onlookers to witness their departure.

In 1762 the Duncan family built the King's Arms on the High Street. Moffat House, designed by John Adam of the famous Adam family of architects, was under construction at the same time for James, Earl of Hopetoun, and as there was a shortage of masons building Moffat House the earl's agent went down to the King's Arms and lured masons working there by offering them a penny more than the eight pence per day they were earning. The building is among the most attractive on the High Street. Viewed from the back the semi-circular tower-like structures at the corners give the impression that perhaps this was intended as the front as the entrance onto High Street is quite plain in comparison. Moffat House became a hotel in the 1930s. There is an entry in the visitors' book from Lord and Lady Baden-Powell complimenting the hotel as 'the most comfortable home we have met with since we left home in the south'.

In the early 1900s Station Road was adequate for horse-drawn traffic to and from the railway station. Later, when motorised traffic entered or left the High Street, the narrowness of the road occasionally caused problems. This led to the reduction of the width of the raised walkway in the centre of the photograph and the removal of the trees bordering the road. The horse and gig are nearing the entrance to the station goods yard and the building bearing the motor garage sign is the Black Bull Hotel, opened in 1568. During the troubled times of the Covenanters in the seventeenth century, John Graham of Claverhouse, 1st Viscount Dundee, alias 'Bluidy Clavers', was billeted here. He stayed for about three years during which time, in 1685, Moffatonians were ordered to take the 'test oath', swearing loyalty to the Crown, in the old kirk yard. Robert Burns also stayed in the establishment on his occasional visits to the district. During one particular sojourn, looking through a window he saw two ladies riding by — one a slim young beauty, the other somewhat larger — prompting him to scratch the following verse on a window pane: 'Ask why God made the gem so small / And why so huge the granite? / Because God meant mankind should set / The higher value on it.'

In the 1920s W.H. Penman owned the service garage bordering Moffat railway station and also the adjacent 'Sportsman's Emporium' on Station Road (now the main road out of town to Beattock; the entrance to Black Bull Close is seen here on the left). Both establishments were kept busy with sales and services as cars, motor cycles and pedal cycles grew ever more popular. The garage also hired out vehicles by the hour, day or week with a comprehensive list of drives to tempt visitors. A sizeable staff of mechanics kept all vehicles in tip-top condition. Following Penman, Tait and Anderson purchased and continued to run the service garage until its closure in the 1960s.

The first sod for the Carlisle to Glasgow section of the Caledonian Railway was cut at a spot near Lockerbie House on 11 October 1845. At 6.30 a.m. on 10 September 1847 the first public train ran from Carlisle to Beattock and on 15 February 1848 the line from Beattock to Glasgow was completed. The branch line from Beattock to Moffat opened on 2 April 1883 at 7.30 a.m., the first sod having being cut by Miss Hope-Johnstone of Marchbank Wood on 13 December 1881. The benefits of the line were felt immediately as a single journey cost two pence and a return three pence, against the six pence cost of a single on the horse-drawn omnibus. There were also savings in the rates for parcels. Time was also saved on the two-mile journey as it only took just over five minutes, whereas the coach took thirteen minutes. Moffat Station was licensed to sell wines and spirits and also had a John Menzies bookstall.

On 11 November 1889 the Moffat Railway Company was officially taken over by Act of Parliament by the Caledonian Railway, which in 1923 was in turn absorbed by the London, Midland and Scottish Railway (LMS). The LMS was nationalised as part of British Railways in 1948. In Caledonian days the passenger service normally comprised a three-coach train – two ancient four-wheelers and an eight-wheeler – and in the early days up to fifteen services ran daily between Moffat and Beattock. Around 1926 a steam rail motor of London and North Western Railway origin appeared on the Moffat branch and took turns on the services with a Drummond '439' and single coach. The steam rail motor No. 10657 was known as the 'Moffat Bus' or the 'Puffer' and was in use until about 1948. This was probably the last British direct-drive steam rail motor with locomotive parts enclosed within the coach body. Thereafter, the service reverted completely to locomotive and coach on a push-pull system. Leaving the Moffat platform, the train soon crossed its first bridge, a small one which allowed access from the Station Park to the Ladyknowe. Then, only a few yards further, it crossed another bridge over the River Annan. The line then bordered the 'Kerr' before crossing a small bridge and the road bridge over the A701 at Hidden Corner, from where it ran through a cutting into the open country before underpassing the A74 Carlisle to Glasgow road. Finally a left-hand curve crossed the River Evan before straightening out for the last quarter mile into the docking platform at Beattock. Although the last timetabled passenger train ran from Moffat at 3.05 p.m. on 6 December 1954, freight continued to be delivered until 6 April 1964. The sad task of pulling up the track fell to a McIntosh '812' 0-6-0, No. 57568. Beattock Station closed on 3 January 1971.

On a Sunday morning in the late 1780s the minister of the old Moffat kirk, the Rev. Alexander Brown, was fortunate enough to have just ushered his congregation out of the building when part of the gable end collapsed. This incident led to the construction of a new parish church, St Andrew's, which was officially opened in 1790. It was built on land gifted by the Earl of Hopetoun and was known as the 'Flying Spur' because of its distinctive weather vane, fashioned to represent his coat of arms (and now atop the war memorial). The church was also known as the 'Father' while the old kirk was referred to as the 'Grandfather'. On 27 April 1885 the church session noted their 'satisfaction that the heritors have resolved to build a new church and manse for the parish'. The laying of the foundation stone of this new church on 8 August 1885 – seen here – was performed by Mr Frederick E. Villiers of Closeburn, Grand Master Mason of Dumfriesshire, aided by officials of the Provincial Grand Lodge, one of whom is holding the time capsule to be placed in the hollow of the stone underneath the foundation stone. The capsule contained nine current coins, newspapers of the day, lists of officials of the parish, a programme of the ceremony and a ground plan of the new church. The new St Andrew's Church opened in 1887.

After being completely rebuilt in 1863, the Buccleuch Hotel became one of the most popular hotels in the town and consequently one of the busiest for coaches. The assortment of excursions to the outlying beauty spots, as advertised in the Moffat guides of the day, encouraged many to reserve a seat and few were disappointed. As well as excursion coaches and cabs, the Buccleuch had for hire post and saddle horses and provided livery stables. Into the twentieth century horse-drawn cabs were in constant use until the more comfortable and speedier motor taxis increased in sufficient numbers to meet the demand.The 'cabbie' in this photograph from around 1930 is James Patterson. He was the last to drive a horse-drawn cab in Moffat and here he has pulled up opposite the British Linen Bank at the north end of the High Street. Constructed in 1855, the building is now called British Linen House.

The northern end of the High Street narrows into Academy Road and in this photograph the original two-roomed academy building of 1834 is in the background, facing the camera. Before it was built the road here was called Townhead. Moffat parish school was established in School Lane in 1803 with John Stevenson as its first master. Previously he had been the master of the grammar school between 1791 and 1799 (this stood at the position on High Street now taken by the war memorial). By 1818 the parish school had 45 pupils while the grammar school had 35. In 1834 they amalgamated to form the academy. In 1873 a school inspector's report stated that on his visit he found the rector, Mr McNeil, in charge of both classes in one room. Seventy-five pupils of the roll of 84 were crammed into the room, which measured 27 by 23 feet, apparently because no other teacher was available at the time. The inspector also reported that the building was in a state of disrepair. Conditions must have greatly improved after the inspector's visit as the new Moffat Academy, built on the same site, wasn't opened until 1934. This itself was replaced by a new academy building on the south-eastern side of the town in 2010.

Beechgrove was named after the row of mature beech trees that bordered the Beechgrove Pleasure Grounds. At a cost of around £600, the three-acre site was laid out in 1870 with tennis and croquet lawns, a bowling green, and there was even a curling pond in the lower level Well tennis court when the temperature dropped low enough. Beechgrove was part of the old Moffat to Edinburgh road that ran along the bottom of the valley before climbing steeply behind Ericstane summit. In 1831 a new road was laid up the slope from Townhead to the Greenhillstairs road and then to the top of the brae. Further progress was made by blasting out the shelf above the Devil's Beef Tub to carry the road round Ericstane. This is the A701. During the lifespan of the Moffat Hydro many hundreds of coaches must have clattered along Beechgrove *en route* to and from Moffat railway station. Over the years, one by one, the beech trees were either felled or storm blown. After one particular storm the building with the notice board on the extreme right of the photograph (a photographer's premises) had to be demolished after a tree crashed through the roof. Today, there is only one tree left standing here – a sycamore.

The first Moffat bowling green was situated in the centre of High Street and in 1826 the green was moved to a new site on the west side of the street. Finally, a green was laid out at the Beechgrove grounds, complete with pavilion, and this is still in use today. In this view from around 1916, Beechwood House overlooks the villas on Beechgrove as a game is in progress. A former member of the bowling club, whose name is still synonymous with both town and club, was Walter Lockerbie. Involved in every aspect of the club, and filling the post of president for a time, it was fitting that when he eventually died on 22 August 1961 it was on Moffat bowling green with a bowl in his hand.

A men's doubles match at the Beechgrove tennis courts, *c.* 1907. The South of Scotland Lawn Tennis Championships have been held in Moffat for over 120 years and many famous players, including Harry Mathieson and Carol Rosser, have graced the tournament over the years. It was quite an occasion when, in 1952, Jim Tuton became the first Moffat-born player to win the singles trophy. He went on to retain the title the following year and was later runner-up on three occasions. He remains the only Moffat-born winner and he also won many other tournaments. He was Scottish team captain and when his playing days began to wane he became national squad coach and a Wimbledon umpire. He also won an award for his contribution to the game from the Lawn Tennis Association of Great Britain, the first award it gave to a Scotsman.

In 1904 Ben Sayers of North Berwick was asked to lay out an eighteen-hole golf course on Coates Hill, on land where the laird – Mr Hope-Johnstone of Annandale – and his friends previously played on a privately owned nine-hole course. Sayers' course was inaugurated on 22 April 1905, the first ball being driven by Lady Younger (women members were allowed!) with a driver presented by Major Mackenzie-Grieve, the captain of the club for that year. Immediately after this ceremony an exhibition match was played by Sir William Younger of the brewing family and Ben Sayers versus their respective sons. The club house seen here is still in use today.

Costing £87,000 to build, the palatial Moffat Hydropathic Hotel opened its doors to the public in April 1878. Built with red sandstone, the magnificent edifice was said to have incorporated into its structure 365 windows – one for every day of the year. The Hydro stood 500 feet above sea level and commanded a view of the loveliest portion of Annandale. It contained over 300 rooms and included a dining hall, drawing room, lounge, billiard room, smoking room, a dark room for amateur photographers and a reading and writing room. There was also a ballroom which doubled as a recreation room and there were large stables and coach houses. The 25 acres of grounds contained tennis and croquet lawns and a putting green. The hotel had all mod cons and boasted a passenger elevator, attributes listed in an advert for the hotel, which also described Moffat's climate as 'salubrious, being particularly beneficial for those suffering from diseases of the chest'.

As the Hydro was originally built to cater for the many hundreds of customers wishing to take the benefit of the 'waters' from the mineral well it is not surprising that the list of baths available was extensive including Turkish, spray, plunge, brine and medicated. There was also an indoor swimming pool. Eventually, however, the fashion for hydropathics waned and, after serving as a convalescence hospital for officers during the First World War, plans to turn the hotel into an institution for tubercular patients in 1921 were turned down. Then, in June that year, the building was destroyed by fire. Dr Huskie, provost of the burgh, gave an account of that night, stating that as the alarm system to summon the firemen of the local brigade was out of action, they had to be roused by knocking on their doors. At about 2 a.m. Dr Huskie arrived at the scene to find the fire engine in position, hose pipes connected to the hydrants, and some firemen on the roof of the building. But all these efforts were to no avail when it was found that there was no water. The Hydro had its own water supply but two months of drought meant that there was not sufficient pressure for the hoses. The Gretna brigade arrived at 3.30 a.m. and soon had water pouring into the building (the appliance carried water and they had longer hoses to reach hydrants that worked) but the flames were too much. The ruins were used by the fire service and Home Guard for training exercises during the Second World War but eventually were demolished.

The Croquet Championship of Scotland was held at the Beechgrove Pleasure Grounds on 18 August 1870, just two weeks after they were officially opened. There were only six entries with the winner, David Johnstone Macfie, awarded the trophy known as the Moffat Mallet. Macfie won again the following year and he featured in every championship from 1872 to 1879, winning the title on two more occasions. 1879 was the last year that the championship was held in Moffat until 1897; it then took place in the town every year until it was moved in 1914 to the Edinburgh Hydropathic. In 1877 the South of Scotland Lawn Tennis Championships were established at Beechgrove, running at the same time as the croquet tournament, and most of the local male croquet players also competed in that.

In the top left of this early photograph of Burnside can be seen the Old Well Road United Presbyterian Church, completed in 1863. The church was demolished in 1967; the hall became the Old Well Theatre. The small cottage just right of centre at the bottom of School Lane was later replaced by a two-storey house and buildings have long since been erected on the left of the road, including St John's Episcopal Church. In 1872 labourers preparing the foundations of this church came across the masonry of an old kiln used for drying grain. The masonry was crude and primitive and the stones, apparently taken from the Mill Burn, were undressed. Lime had been sparingly used in the mortar and the form of the kiln was circular or oval with a chamber about twelve feet across. The Burnside kiln must have been of considerable importance at one time but no information has emerged about when it fell into disuse. The part of Moffat comprising fields between High Street and the Mill Burn was known as Kiln Knowes until some time into the nineteenth century. The burn itself is named after a meal mill which later became Taylor and Smith's sawmill and joinery business, operating between 1935 and 1965.

By 1900 Burnside had changed considerably. St John's Church was originally made from corrugated plates of galvanised iron attached to a wooden frame on a brick foundation. Its construction was funded by a Liverpool merchant, J. Toulmin Lawrence, who for several years rented the house at Craigieburn Estate as his summer and autumn residence. The church had accommodation for 300 and was opened on 7 July 1872. Locally, it was known as the 'tin tabernacle' and the 'iron church'. It had a very fine organ built by the well-known organ builder Henry 'Father' Willis. The church was rebuilt in 1951 and still has the organ.

Mr Hood moved to Moffat from Glasgow in 1857 and opened his photographic studio on Well Road, next to Taylor and Smith's sawmill. He married his assistant, Emily, and the family was completed when their daughter Emilie was born. His work involved mostly taking family portraits but he also took photographs for the Hydro's illustrated brochures. Mrs Hood took over the business after the death of her husband, and established a branch in Lockerbie. In turn, Emilie later succeeded to the business.

The great snow storm of late 1947 is one of the worst Moffat has suffered; it was also quite unusual due to the fact that the winds behind the snow caused deep drifts on one side of local streets while leaving the opposite sides relatively snow free. On the east side of High Street the snow at the Union Bank Building (now home to Pinocchio's toy and craft shop) sloped in such a fashion from roof to the road that a tunnel was excavated for access. The Holm road was cleared by a gang of local volunteers who, when standing on top of the drifts, could touch the telephone wires. Much of the snow cleared from local streets was dumped in the Annandale Field and took many weeks to thaw. Hood's studio appears to have got off lightly with frost more of a problem. By that time the studio had amassed so many glass photographic plates that the sheer weight necessitated extra support under the storage area.

The crossroads at Holmend, pictured around 1915. The road to Selkirk ahead leads out of the village to the Grey Mare's Tail, while on the left is Ballplay Road and, on the right, Queensberry Terrace, part of the Old Carlisle Road. This view is largely unchanged apart from the removal of the trees and empty area on the left; this has since been taken by small factory units, the Moffat Fire Station and the base for Moffat Mountain Rescue.

In 1633 Moffat's transformation from a poor village to prosperous spa town began when one Rachel Whiteford discovered a sulphurous spring while out walking in the hills to the north-east of Moffat. The so-called healing properties of the water were later exploited by a Moffat physician, Dr Hunter, and by 1760 he had improved access by building a bridge over the Hindgill Burn and extending the small shed which had been built over the well. By 1827 the Baths Hall (later becoming the Town Hall) was catering to the many visitors who came to bathe in the 'healing waters' which were piped from the well to the hall. Business and trading improved in Moffat throughout the 1800s, culminating in the opening of the Hydro, which also had water piped from the well. Standing in the doorway of Dr Hunter's building (albeit altered to create a more closed-in room) with drinking glasses at the ready, the well attendant is ready to greet early morning visitors.

Farmland known as the Ballplay separated the fine villas of Ballplay Road from the main part of the town. Right of centre in this photograph is Holm Park, the home of Warriston School, while the house called Warriston is to its right. In later years Holm Park was used as a mushroom farm and riding centre before being boarded up. It was subsequently converted into flats. The Ballplay itself has long since been built over with housing.

Warriston College – later Warriston School for Boys - was established around 1879 and originally based in the house Burnbraes on Well Road (now the Well Road Centre). It was named after Archibald Johnstone, Lord Warriston, a famous seventeenth-century lawyer who was active during Covenanting times. In 1892 it was advertising itself as a 'high class boarding school for boys', offering special classes for military or naval schools, the civil service, and medical and law examinations. It moved to Holm Park in 1899 and, while it only had five pupils at that time, over the years it developed into one of Scotland's leading prep schools. It was closed for the duration of the Second World War and later moved to the houses St Ninian's and Dundanion in the main part of the town. The school closed in 1979. The swimming pool was behind Holm Park while the school's playing fields were on the south side of the Holm road, an area now taken by the rugby club and the recently built secondary school.

WARRISTON PLAYING FIELDS, MOFFAT.

DIVING STAGE AND WATER SHUTE,
THE SWIMMING BATH AT WARRISTON SCHOOL, MOFFAT.

Near the junction of Dundanion Road and Old Well Road is the entry into Hartfell Crescent, a row of large nineteenth-century houses. At the far end of the crescent a narrow path leads to Well Road via Haywood Road and anyone choosing to walk to the well by this route could admire the tidy and productive gardens, belonging to the houses, on the gently sloping ground on the opposite side of the road. At the same junction some walkers preferred to carry on past Larchhill House and on to, then round, the Gallow Hill. At one time gallows had been erected on this wooded slope but they were never used.

Despite having spent his working life at sea, Albert Horatio Walker and his family left Burntisland in 1920 to take over Rogermoor Farm and members of the Walker family have been in residence there ever since. Rogermoor was typical of many other Annandale farms at that time, depending on both dairy and arable farming. Farming didn't appeal to Albert's oldest son, Albert Jnr, who left the country and went to work in Malaya as a rubber planter. Albert had two sons: Chris (who was known in the town as the local strongman) left and settled to farming down south while Maurice eventually took over Rogermoor, running a successful dairy business while the farm diversified with root crops, oats and hay.

Previous to the formation of Coxhill Duck Farm by Major David Ralston in 1925, this area one and a half miles south-east of the town down the Old Carlisle Road was a nine-hole golf course. In 1936 a cobbled floor was discovered along with various items that indicated that the site once was a smiddy. In the eighteenth century this was Robin Tamson's smiddy, which was associated with Robert Burns who visited the inn or change house, Nethermill, on the Old Carlisle Road. Between Netherhill and the site of the old smiddy runs the Frenchland Burn and this is mentioned in a verse of the song, 'Robin Tamson's Smiddy' which runs, 'The smiddy stands ayont the burn that wimples thro' the Clachan an ilka time I pass the door, I canna keep fae laughin'. The reason for the laughter lay in the story which the ballad goes on to relate: 'My mither ment my auld breeks. An, wow, but they were duddie, o! She sent me to get shod the mare at Robin Tamson's smiddy, O!' On 20 July 1940 Moffat had its first experience of modern war when three German bombs fell and exploded at the duck farm. The bombs left three large craters near the duck houses, but these remained intact without any loss or anyone being injured. By 1954 Coxhill was fattening 10,000 Aylesbury ducklings every year and by 1966 the *Scottish Farmer* reported Coxhill as 'Scotland's biggest duck farm: fattens 25,000 yearly'. After over fifty years in business Coxhill was forced into closure by EU regulations in 1980.

The classical beauty of Dumcrieff House is a far cry from the defensive tower and hamlet of that name which was owned by the Murrays of Cockpool from 1482. A small two-storey house was built around 1684 and the property later passed through several hands before it was bought in 1806 by Dr John Rogerson, who had been personal physician to Catherine the Great of Russia. Rogerson built the present mansion in 1821. The estate then passed to the doctor's only daughter who married the 9th Lord Rollo and from 1836 to 1916 John Rogerson Rollo, 10th Lord Rollo, was owner of the estate. It was then owned by a local reverend for many years and passed through further hands until the current owners, who have ancestral links to the estate dating back to the fifteenth century, bought it in 2008. From 1783 to 1784 John Loudon Macadam of road-making fame rented Dumcrieff and one of his road rollers still stands in the grounds. Macadam died in Moffat in 1836, while *en route* to his later home in England. His headstone can be seen in Moffat's old kirkyard.

Woodfoot Bridge over the River Annan at Woodfoot Farm, about a mile below the 'Meetings of the Waters' (the rivers Annan and Evan and the Moffat Water). The Woodfoot stretch of the river, especially at the 'Plum', a pool popular with anglers, was a favourite spot for the sea trout night fisher. From June to September there would always be a row of anglers' bicycles parked near the bridge and also at the 'Meetings of the Waters', with anglers chatting at the riverside anticipating the 'gloaming'. At this time, in well-running water at 'Woodhead Scar', it was possible to land half a dozen good fish before pedalling home, but stocks are much lower these days and this hasn't been achieved for many years. From September to the end of the season the salmon fisher came into his own and many neighbours benefited from a day's fishing, when a brace of salmon had been tempted by a fly lure or even a humble worm.

The River Evan runs down Evan Valley from its source, just beyond Lytle Clyde, and as it flows the few miles to the 'Meetings of the Waters', where it joins with the River Annan and Moffat Water, it is added to by streams such as Bidhouse Burn, Cloffin Burn and Garpol Water. The road, river and main railway line from Glasgow to Carlisle run close together all the way down the valley from the Harthope Viaduct to Beattock railway station, where the banking engines required to assist the heavy trains up to Beattock Summit were based.

The Evan Valley from Greenhillstairs during the upgrading of this part of the A74 dual carriageway to motorway, which took place between 1997 and 1999. Forty years after the route was last upgraded, the sheer volume of traffic in both directions necessitated further improvements with the result being the construction of the six-lane M74 motorway. During construction a service road had to be accessible – an A.P.R. (all-purpose road) – and this temporary bridge over the motorway allowed access to the A.P.R. from Greenhillstairs. The columns were to become part of a permanent overpass across the motorway. The River Evan's course was slightly diverted at this point until construction was complete, although the railway line was unchanged. By this time the line had long been electrified and heavy passenger and freight trains no longer needed a banking engine to assist them up the ten-mile gradient to Beattock Summit.

The Devil's Beef Tub on the Moffat to Edinburgh Road was once used by border reivers to conceal cattle and contraband before moving them into Tweedsmuir. James Welsh, the 'Bairn of Tweedhope-Foot', well known for his huge build and strength, was in the company of covenanter John Hunter when the latter was murdered at the Tub on Corehead by Colonel James Douglas and his dragoons in 1685. Hunter and Welsh fled on foot up the steep hill behind the house. Out of breath, Hunter told Welsh to go on and save himself and minutes later the dragoons caught up and shot him. Welsh got through the Skailstep and on to the moor above then made it to his aunt's home at Carterhope. She put some old clothes about him and sat him down by the fire, and when the soldiers arrived the old woman gave Welsh a slap on the shoulder and told him to 'get up and haud the sodgers' horses.' The dragoons searched the house in vain, then rode off, never realising Welsh was there all the time. There is a monument to the memory of Hunter on the lip of the Tub by the roadside of the A701.

An excursion to the Garpol Glen in the early 1900s was extremely popular. The Garpol had much to offer in the way of scenic beauty and panoramic views and there was also a 'spa' within the glen. There were two cascading waterfalls, the upper fall and the lower fall which had a conveniently placed bridge. Close by are the ruins of the Old Auchencas, a castle dating from the time of Robert the Bruce. At the top of the Glen, the woodland glade had summer seats conveniently sited among the shrubs, with well maintained paths throughout.

Lochhouse Tower, built in the 1500s, is situated about a mile from Moffat on the Beattock Road. It was referred to as the 'Echo Tower', as a call within it in the right direction produced a perfect echo. The echo disappeared when the building was renovated and reroofed. The tower has a romantic association with Frenchlands Tower because, in the late sixteenth century, the Laird of Frenchlands and Lilias Johnstone from Lochhouse were lovers. The couple were often seen walking the bank of the River Evan together and hoped to eventually marry. Lilias's brother, the Laird of Corehead, had no great liking for the Laird of Frenchlands and forbade his sister to marry, though the couple continued to walk out together. At the Battle of Dryfe Sands on 7 December 1592, the last clan battle fought in Scotland, Corehead Johnstone was killed. Lilias, knowing that she was now free to marry, visited Frenchlands, only to find that, tired of waiting, the Laird had married the Laird of Breconside's daughter. Although Lilias was extremely beautiful she never married and it is said that she pined for her lost love and died of a broken heart.

The close proximity of Moffat to the English border necessitated the construction of stone peel defensive towers during the fifteenth and sixteenth centuries to protect the locals and their goods and livestock from both English raiders and marauding Scottish clans. At least half a dozen of these towers were within a few miles' radius of the town, but only Lochhouse Tower on the Moffat to Beattock road is still inhabited today. The remains in this photograph are of Frenchlands Tower, a mile or so from Moffat on the Selkirk Road. The French family is said to have originally occupied the lands in this vicinity in 1428 and the tower remained in the family until 1748 when it was sold to Lord Elliock. He owned it for about forty years before selling it to Dr Rogerson of Dumcrieff, who added it to his estate although it did eventually fall into neglect.

High on a hill to the west of Moffat stands a monument to the twelfth-century Knights of St John (The Knights Templar). The monument, an arched window, is all that remains of their chapel which dates to that period. Although the Annandale Knights' main settlement was at Chapel Farm, much of the land on both sides of the River Annan was farmed by them.

The Moffat Gaslight Company was formed in 1837. On 27 February 1838 Andrew Liddel and Co. of Glasgow agreed to supply the company with all apparatus, pipes and brickwork for the sum of £615. The gasworks entry was from Holm Street and up until Moffat railway station opened in 1883 coal was delivered by horse-drawn carts. The station's goods yard was adjacent to the gasworks with a coal siding for use by it and coal merchants. Although coal was now delivered by mechanical means it still had to be unloaded by hand into a small two-wheel cart employed by the gasworks. The bill below is for the sale of coal from the Hydro to the gas company. It was paid on 17 June 1921, just before the Hydro fire.

MOFFAT HYDRO HOTEL.

"Where smiling Spring its earliest visit pays,
And parting Summer's lingering bloom delays."

Telephone No. 8 Moffat.
Telegrams: "Hydro," Moffat.

MOFFAT, 13th May 1921

8tons 2 Cwts Best House Coal @ 50/ per Ton £ 20 - 5/

Messrs
The Moffat Gas Co